Cello Time Starters

a beginner book for cello

Kathy and David Blackwell

Illustrations by

Martin Remphry

MUSIC DEPARTMENT

OXFORD
UNIVERSITY PRESS

Great Clarendon Street, Oxford OX2 6DP, England

ISBN 978-0-19-336583-4

Music and text origination by Julia Bovee
Printed in Great Britain on acid-free paper by
Halstan & Co. Ltd, Amersham, Bucks.

Welcome to **Cello Time Starters**. You'll find:

- Lots of tunes to sing and then play
- Lively audio tracks to listen and play along to
- Quizzes to do—grab a pencil
- 'Super listener' games—get your ears ready
- 'Be a composer' activities—get creative!

What you'll need:

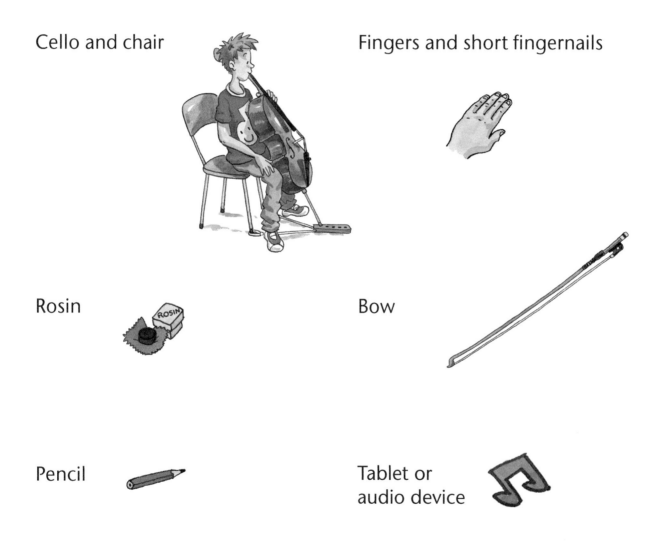

Cello and chair

Fingers and short fingernails

Rosin

Bow

Pencil

Tablet or
audio device

Got these? Let's get started.

Tune your strings to audio tracks 71–4 (A, D, G, C).

This book belongs to _____

Feel the beat

1 🎧 Music has a steady beat, can you feel it in your feet?

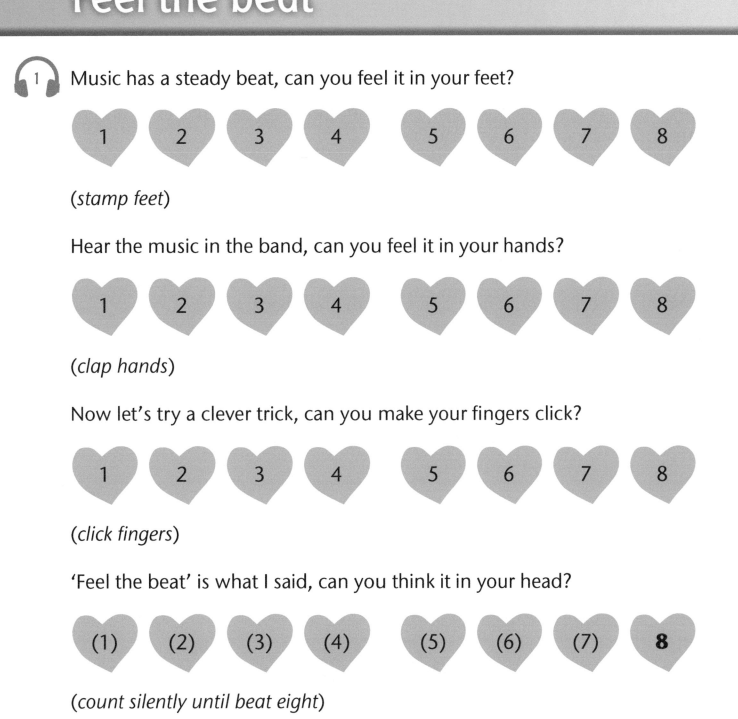

(*stamp feet*)

Hear the music in the band, can you feel it in your hands?

(*clap hands*)

Now let's try a clever trick, can you make your fingers click?

(*click fingers*)

'Feel the beat' is what I said, can you think it in your head?

(*count silently until beat eight*)

Music has a steady beat or pulse. Just like your heartbeat, it keeps going all the way through a song or tune. A fast tune will have a fast beat and a slower tune a slower beat.

Tap a steady beat and chant the words of a song you know well. Keep tapping all the way through.

Know your cello

Song time

Sing these words to the tune of 'Head, shoulders, knees, and toes' and point to the different parts of your instrument.

Scroll, shoulders, strings, and bridge, strings and bridge,
Scroll, shoulders, strings, and bridge, strings and bridge,
* And the pegs and spike and the fingerboard,
Scroll, shoulders, strings, and bridge, strings and bridge.

* **Verse 2**: And the nut and *f* holes and the tail-piece,

Picture time

Draw a line from each word to the correct part of the cello.

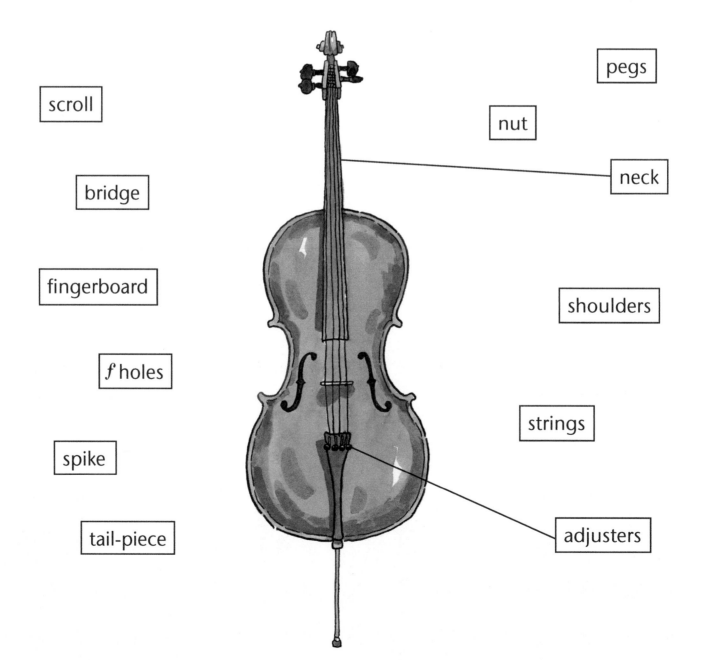

scroll

pegs

nut

neck

bridge

fingerboard

shoulders

f holes

strings

spike

tail-piece

adjusters

3 Get-ready rag

Sit up straight on the front half of your chair and get ready to do each of the actions along with the audio track. Start with your cello upright at arm's length. Once your cello is in place, do actions 5–8 while you move to the music.

1. Sit up tall and straight,

2. Tap your feet apart,

3. On your left-hand side,

Are your feet flat on the floor?

4. Now it's time to start.

5. Feel the beat: sway on the spot, left and right.

6. Swinging hammock: swing your elbows.

7. High jump: tap your left hand on the strings or the wood either side of the fingerboard.

8. Long jump: slide your left hand up and down the fingerboard.

First sounds

In these tunes, pluck the open strings with your right-hand fingers. Make a big circle in the air with your right arm, like this:

 Sway and strum

Sway gently from side to side in time to the music while you strum the strings.

| 1 | 2 | 3 | 1 | 2 | 3 |

Strum...   strum...   etc.

 At the zoo

Listen to the sound of each string, then play the note pizzicato—that means plucking.

Listen   *Play and chant*

A	for alligators		A	for alligators
D	for dolphins		D	for dolphins
G	for gorillas		G	for gorillas
C	for camels		C	for camels

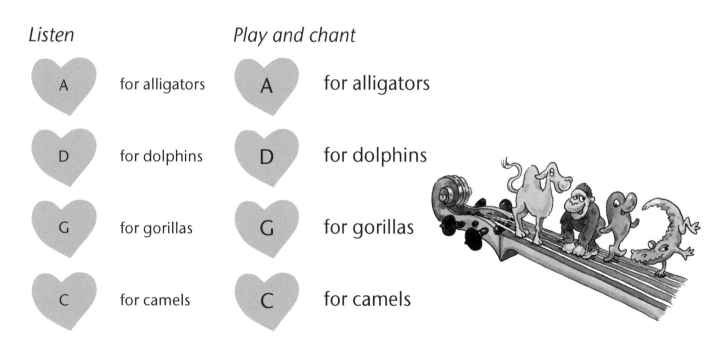

Chant
That's what we have in our zoo. Yeah!

6 Swing, swing, swing your arm

Sing and then play this piece to the tune of 'Row, row, row your boat'.

G		G		G		D	
Swing,	swing,	swing your	arm,	as we	sing this	song.	

x2

G		G		D		G	
Swing it	out and	swing it	in, we'll	swing it	all day	long.	

Is your arm swinging away from each string?

7 Flying around

C			A		
Swing	with	your	arm	as	you

D			G		
pluck	ev	-	'ry	string.	

C			A		
Fly	- ing	a	- round	is	a

D			G		
won	- der	- ful	thing!		

Repeat once and end with a final C.

7

First tunes

Play these tunes pizzicato, placing your thumb
on the edge of the fingerboard.

 8 **Counting beats**

Play this piece four times, once with each string.

Chant
Counting beats is for the best, play four Cs* then count four rests.

Play x4

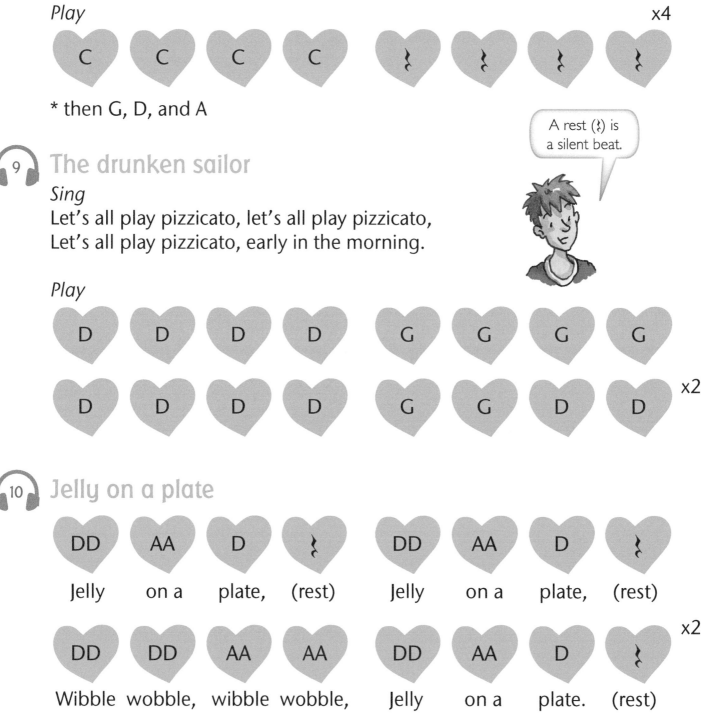

| C | C | C | C | ∤ | ∤ | ∤ | ∤ |

* then G, D, and A

> A rest (∤) is
> a silent beat.

9 **The drunken sailor**

Sing
Let's all play pizzicato, let's all play pizzicato,
Let's all play pizzicato, early in the morning.

Play

| D | D | D | D | G | G | G | G |

| D | D | D | D | G | G | D | D | x2

10 **Jelly on a plate**

| DD | AA | D | ∤ | DD | AA | D | ∤ |
| Jelly | on a | plate, | (rest) | Jelly | on a | plate, | (rest) |

x2

| DD | DD | AA | AA | DD | AA | D | ∤ |
| Wibble | wobble, | wibble | wobble, | Jelly | on a | plate. | (rest) |

Super listener

When you can sing and then play 'Jelly on a plate' really well, try a lower version starting on the G string. Then play an even lower version—which string will you begin on?

Be a composer

1. Make up your own tune by playing the pattern of the following words on your open strings. Tap a steady beat and say the words through a few times before you start.

'I hear footsteps on the street.
Someone's there with great big feet!'

2. Invent your own tune using notes from the boxes. Write your tune in the heartbeat spaces—one box per heartbeat—and then play it from start to finish.

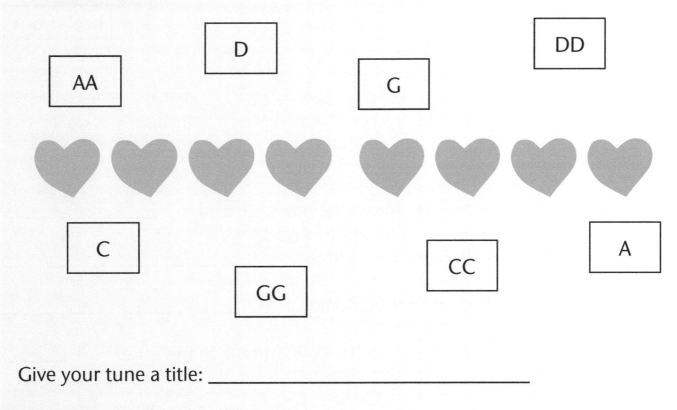

Give your tune a title: _____

Know your bow

Song time

Sing these words along with the audio track and point to the different parts of the bow.

1. There's the point and the heel and the stick in between,
   Don't touch the hair to keep it clean.

2. Turn the screw to the right to make the hair tight,
   Rosin the bow and off we go.

3. Turn the screw to the left to loosen the bow,
   That's what we do when it's time to go.

Picture time

Draw a line from each word to the correct part of the bow.

stick   point (tip)

screw   heel (frog)

            hair

Quiz time

What am I?

You turn me to loosen and tighten the hair of the bow: _____

I'm part of the bow that you don't touch: _____

You rub me on the hair before you play: _____

You'll find the heel at one end of the bow and me at the other end: _____

Yo bow!

Get ready to perform this bow-hold rap by holding the middle of the stick with your left hand. The tip of the bow will point to your left.

1. Shake your right hand to the ground,
   Wiggle those fingers all around.

2. Hang your fingers right over the stick,
   Slightly apart now, that's the trick.

3. Keep your fingers hanging down,
   Let them point right to the ground.

4. Bend your thumb and bring it round,
   Keep it curved to make a great sound.

5. Yo bow! Yo bow!
   To the left, to the right, and off we go.

6. Yo bow! Yo bow!
   Up and down and off we go.

Is your little finger curving over the stick?

7. Yo bow! Yo bow!
   Round and round and off we go.

8. Yo bow! Yo bow!
   Side to side and off we go.

Down- and up-bow signs

⊓ This is a down-bow sign—pull your right hand away from the strings.

Ⅴ This is an up-bow sign—push your right hand up towards the strings.

Play this pattern on each open string: ⊓ Ⅴ ⊓ Ⅴ
down up down up

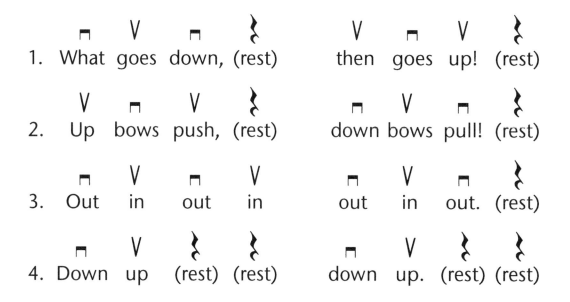

Move the bow up and down, keeping it parallel to the bridge.

Following the signs

Choose one of these patterns and play it a few times on an open string.

⊓ Ⅴ ⊓ ⸾ Ⅴ ⊓ Ⅴ ⸾
1. What goes down, (rest)   then goes up! (rest)

Ⅴ ⊓ Ⅴ ⸾ ⊓ Ⅴ ⊓ ⸾
2. Up bows push, (rest)   down bows pull! (rest)

⊓ Ⅴ ⊓ Ⅴ ⊓ Ⅴ ⊓ ⸾
3. Out in out in   out in out. (rest)

⊓ Ⅴ ⸾ ⸾ ⊓ Ⅴ ⸾ ⸾
4. Down up (rest) (rest)   down up. (rest) (rest)

Try the same patterns on your rosin. Make sure the bow moves and not the rosin!

Now play the tunes on page 8 arco—that means with the bow. For 'The drunken sailor', change the words to 'Let's all play arco'.

Rhythm zone 1: walk, jogging

'walk'
crotchet (or quarter-note)

'jogging'
quavers (or eighth-notes)

- Clap the rhythms below, saying 'walk' for each ♩ and 'jogging' for each ♫
- Ask someone to tap the beat while you clap the rhythms, and then swap.
- Choose one row of beats (a bar or measure) and play that rhythm on each open string. For Set 1, count a steady **1**-2-3-4, **1**-2-3-4 before you start. For Set 2, count **1**-2-3, **1**-2-3.
- Finally, play each ♩ on the G string and each ♫ on the D string, or choose two other strings that are next to each other.

$\frac{4}{4}$ is a **time signature**. It means four ♩ beats in each bar.

What do you think $\frac{3}{4}$ means?

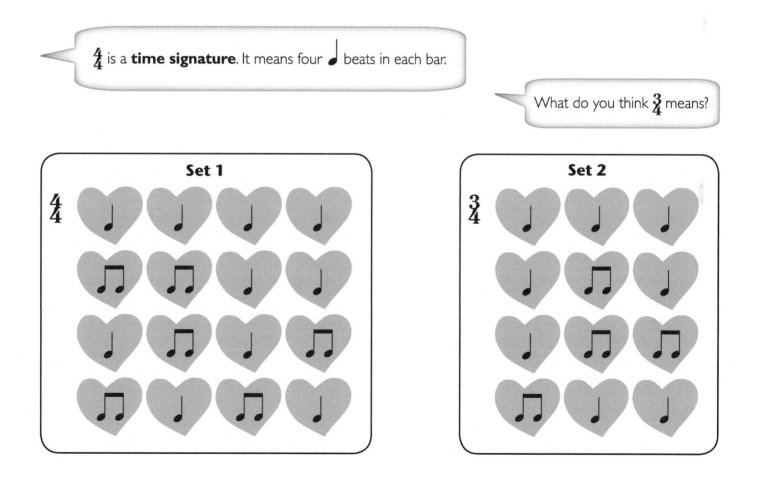

 Super listener

Listen to track 13, 'Echo calypso', and copy back the rhythms on the D and A strings.

Notes on the stave

14 Open-string rap

Chant

Cello strings from high to low, let me tell you how they go.
First there's A then D then G, way down low you'll find the C.
A D G C. Way down low you'll find the C.

Play each string from high to low, start with A and down you go.

Play

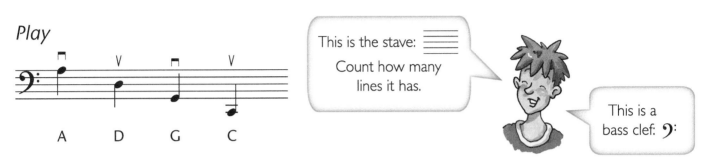

A   D   G   C

This is the stave: ▤
Count how many
lines it has.

This is a
bass clef: 𝄢

Chant

Play each string from low to high, start with C then reach for the sky!

Play

C   G   D   A

Quiz time

Draw the correct open string above each letter to spell the words as notes.

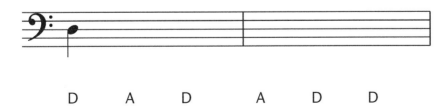

D   A   D   A   D   D

What words do these notes spell? Fill in the name of each string to find out.

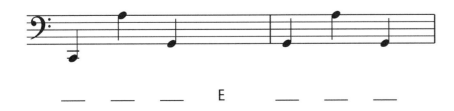

___   ___   ___   E   ___   ___   ___

14

Walk and jogging tunes

15 At the zoo

Be a composer

Make up your own rhythms using the open strings. Think of something beginning with each letter and then play the pattern of the words on each string. You could use the names of friends or different places as starting points. Write your words in the spaces below:

A for _____

D for _____

G for _____

C for _____

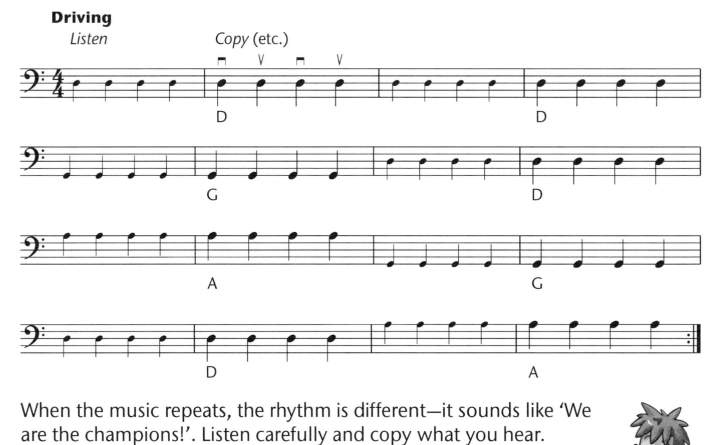

Driving

Listen   *Copy* (etc.)

When the music repeats, the rhythm is different—it sounds like 'We are the champions!'. Listen carefully and copy what you hear.

17 **Mini Mozart**

This is a repeat sign:

Mozart, arr. KB/DB

Gracefully

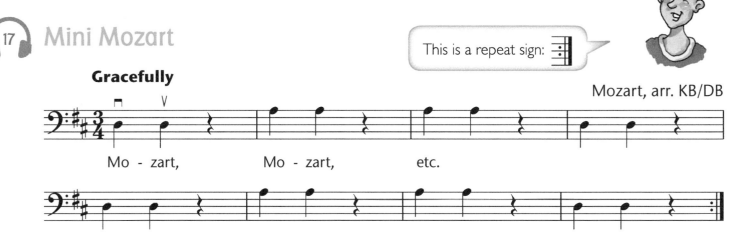

Mo - zart,   Mo - zart,   etc.

Try these rhythm variations:

Wolf-gang A - ma - de - us,   Wolf-gang A - ma - de - us,   etc.

Walk   jog - ging walk,   walk   jog - ging walk,   etc.

Pull   to   the   tip then   push   to   the   heel then

Boogie band

With energy

Boo-gie on the o-pen D, boo-gie on the o-pen G, boo-gie on the o-pen D,

boo-gie on the A. Boo-gie on the o-pen D, boo-gie on the o-pen G,

Shout

boo-gie on the D then G. Yeah!

19 Rhythm train

Verse 1

Lively

Listen   *Copy* (etc.)

O-ver-night ex-press train, O-ver-night ex-press train, etc.

Verse 2

Listen   *Copy*   etc.

All a-board, all a-board, All a-board, all a-board,

End with some
train whistle sounds!

Verse 3

Listen   *Copy*   etc.

Train whis-tle, train whis-tle, Train whis-tle, train whis-tle,

20 Super listener

Listen to track 20 and play 'Rhythm train' using your C and G strings.

Sound effects

 Mr Pizzicato and friends

Sing the words and play the notes in each verse.

Verse 1

Mr Pizzicato likes to pluck the string, he puts his finger here and he lets it ring:

Mr Pizzicato likes to pluck the string.

Verse 2

Mr Arco has a great bow-hold, he strokes the strings and it sounds so bold:

Mr Arco has a great bow-hold.

Verse 3

Mr Col Legno likes to use the wood, he bounces very gently and it sounds real good:

Mr Col Legno likes to use the wood.

Verse 4

Mr Tremolo likes to shiver with his bow, so he puts it near the tip and this is how it goes:

Mr Tremolo likes to shiver with his bow.

> End the song with tremolo on the D string.

Use your new tremolo skills to play a spooky version of 'The drunken sailor' on page 8. Change the words to 'Let's all play with tremolo bowing'.

String-crossing tunes

In these string-crossing tunes, watch your elbow swing *down* when you play a lower string and *up* when you play a higher string.

22 Happy Haydn

19

Rhythm zone 2: slow-walk

Say and clap the rhythm below while a friend or teacher taps the beat, and then swap over. Remember to count and feel two beats for each ♩

'slow - walk'
minim (or half-note)

Walk   walk   walk   walk,   slow - walk   slow - walk,   etc.

24 Classical sounds

Verse 1

Gracefully

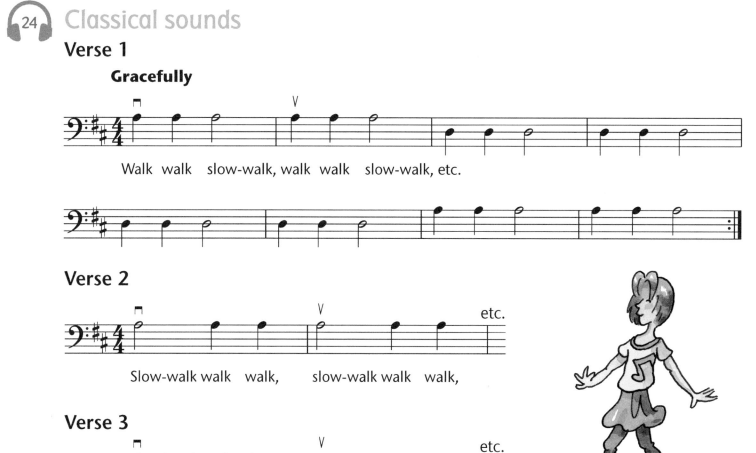

Walk   walk   slow-walk,   walk   walk   slow-walk,   etc.

Verse 2

Slow-walk walk   walk,   slow-walk walk   walk,

Verse 3

At the heel then slow-walk, at the tip then slow-walk,

25 Super listener

Listen to track 25 and play 'Classical sounds' using your D and G strings. The first note will be open D.

Slow-walk tunes

26 Raindrops

Gently

Rain-drops fall   from the sky,   ground is wet,   so am I.

On my head,   on my knees,   wish I had my wel - lies!

27 Swing band

Lively, swing

Swing   your   el - bow   as you cross the   string,

Swing   your   el - bow   as you cross the   string,

1.   *Chant*

See - saw   bow - ing, that's the   thing!   One more time now!

2.   **Slower**   trem.

thing!   Swing   it,   yeah!

Remember
Mr Tremolo!

Left-hand pizzicato

In these tunes you'll need to use left-hand pizzicato. When you see the **+** sign, pluck the string with your left-hand 3rd or 4th finger.

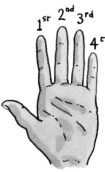

28 Chinese festival

Steadily

29 Popcorn

First sing the song and play left-hand pizzicato in the 'Pop! Bang!' bars. Then play with right-hand pizzicato or arco for the rest of the tune, but keep using your left hand for 'Pop! Bang!'.

Happily

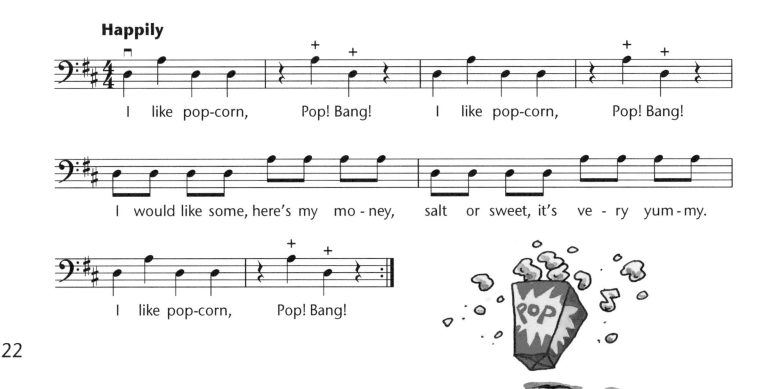

I like pop-corn, Pop! Bang! I like pop-corn, Pop! Bang!

I would like some, here's my mo-ney, salt or sweet, it's ve-ry yum-my.

I like pop-corn, Pop! Bang!

22

Finger jogging time

Four joggers

Say this rhyme and tap each fingertip in turn on your left-hand thumb.

4th finger:	Four	jog - gers	out	one	day,		one	fell	down	and	lost	his	way.
3rd finger:	Three	jog - gers	out	one	day,		**two**	fell	down	and	lost	their	way.
1st finger:	One	jog - ger	out	one	day,		he	fell	down	and	lost	his	way.
0 fingers:	No	jog - gers	out	to - day!		(Stop!)

Super listener

Listen to track 30 and play 'Four joggers' on your D string, starting with your 4th finger. Remember to lift your 3rd and 2nd fingers off together.

Sporty rhythms

Shape up your left-hand fingers on the D string. Choose a sporty rhythm from below and play it on each fingered note and on the open D: 43–1–0.

Walk   walk   slow - walk,

Jog-ging walk   jog-ging walk,

Rea - dy, stea - dy, go   now,

Quick   run - ner, fast   sprint-er,

Also try playing up the notes from the open string: 0–1–34.

Finger jogging tunes

You can play these tunes on any string, but if you play with the audio track, make sure you use the string shown.

31 Fingers and feet (D string)

$\frac{4}{4}$

33	33	44	44	33	33	11	11
From our	fingers	to our	feet, we	always	keep a	steady	beat, we

33	33	44	44	33	11	0	
keep it	going	in a	song if	notes are	short or	long_____.	

(Stamp feet eight times, then repeat.)

32 Roller coaster (D string)

$\frac{4}{4}$

4	4	33	33	11	11	0	0
Speed -	ing	roller	coaster,	spinning	me a -	round.	I'm

11	11	3	3	44	44	4	𝄽
feeling	very	diz -	zy	so far	from the	ground.	(rest)

(Make circles in the air with the bow, then repeat.)

33 String band (A string)

$\frac{4}{4}$

3	1	0	𝄽	3	1	0	𝄽
Big	cel -	los,	(rest)	big	cel -	los,	(rest)

00	00	11	11	3	1	0	𝄽
double	basses,	vio -	lins, and	big	cel -	los.	(rest)

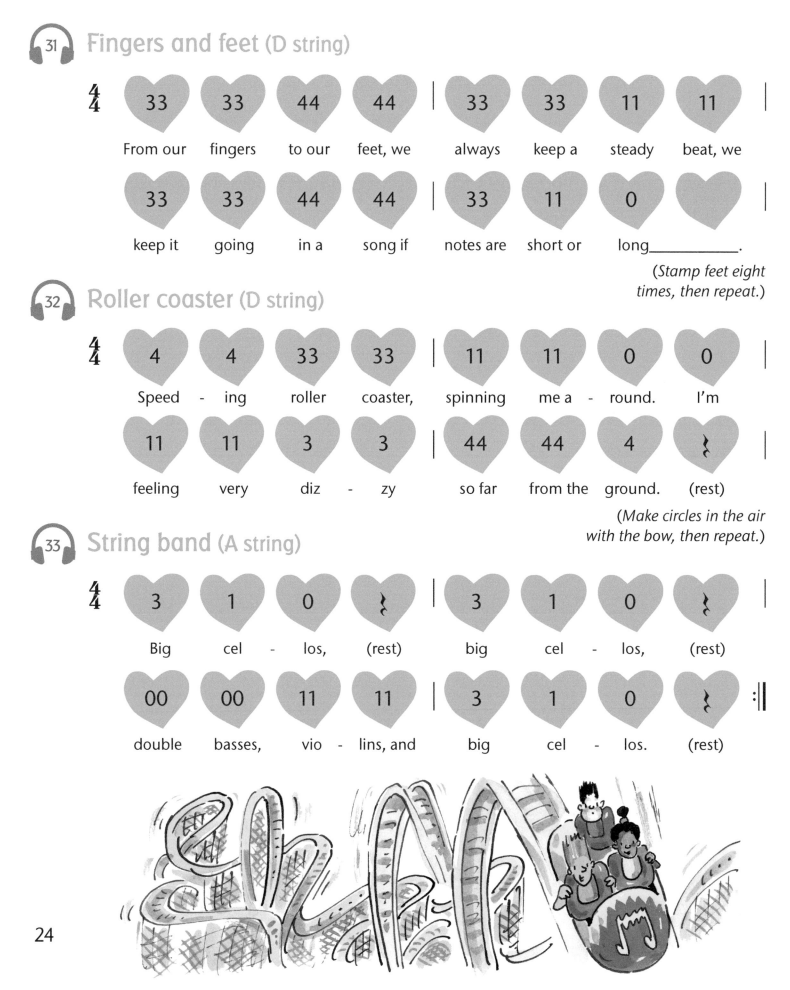

24

34 Rain, rain (A string)

$\frac{4}{4}$ **4** **1** **44** **1** | **44** **11** **44** **1** :‖

Rain, rain, go a - way, please don't rain on Satur - day.

35 Twinkle, twinkle, little star

This tune uses two different strings—a lower one and a higher one. Audio track 35 is played on the D and A strings.

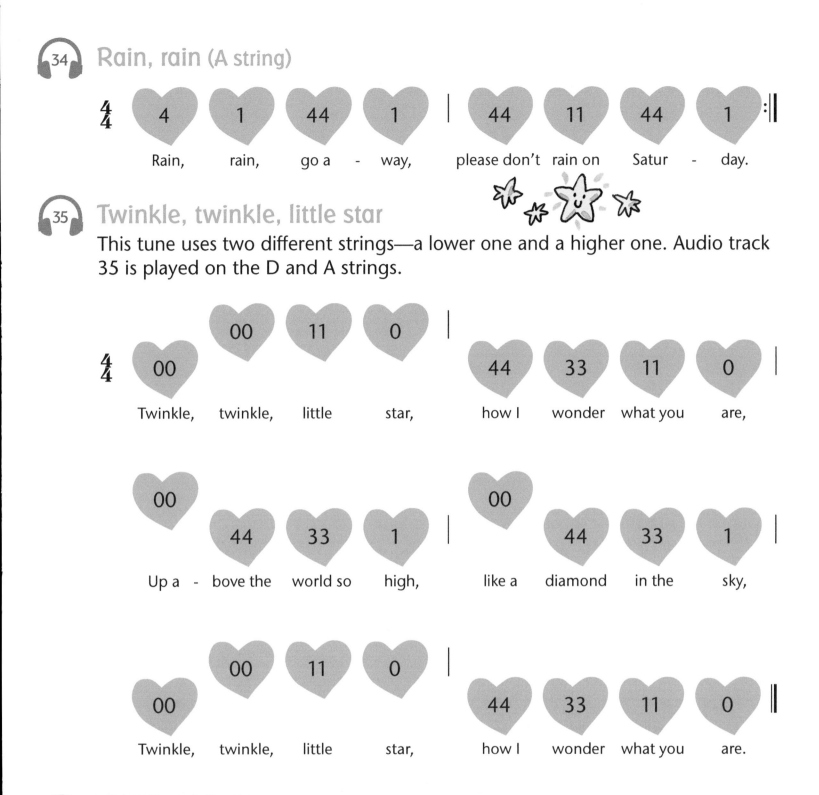

$\frac{4}{4}$ **00** **00** **11** **0** |

Twinkle, twinkle, little star,

44 **33** **11** **0** |

how I wonder what you are,

00 **44** **33** **1** |

Up a - bove the world so high,

00 **44** **33** **1** |

like a diamond in the sky,

00 **00** **11** **0** |

Twinkle, twinkle, little star,

44 **33** **11** **0** ‖

how I wonder what you are.

36 Super listener

Listen to track 36 and play 'Twinkle, twinkle, little star' starting on the G string.

Be a composer

Using the words below, make up your own tune using the left-hand fingers. Tap a steady beat and say the words through a few times before you start.

'Deep in the jungle, what do you see?
Alligators, alligators after me!'

D-string notes

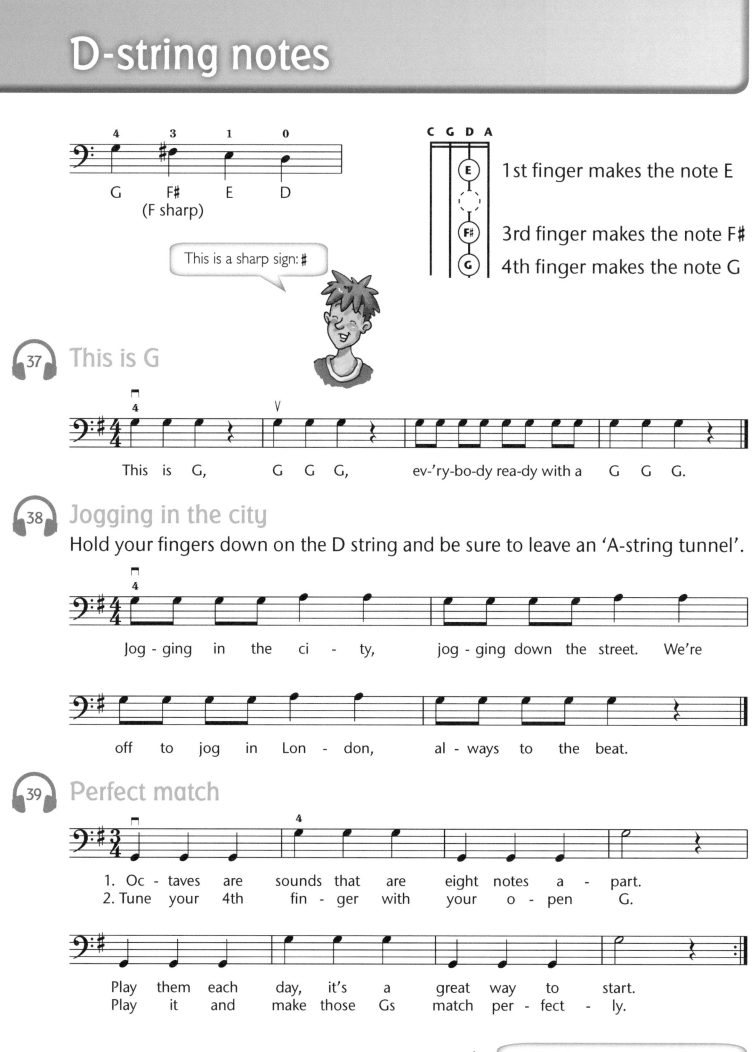

4   3   1   0
G   F#   E   D
   (F sharp)

This is a sharp sign: ♯

C G D A
1st finger makes the note E
3rd finger makes the note F♯
4th finger makes the note G

37 This is G

This is G,   G G G,   ev-'ry-bo-dy rea-dy with a   G G G.

38 Jogging in the city

Hold your fingers down on the D string and be sure to leave an 'A-string tunnel'.

Jog - ging   in   the   ci - ty,   jog - ging down the street.   We're

off   to   jog   in   Lon - don,   al - ways   to   the   beat.

39 Perfect match

1. Oc - taves   are   sounds that   are   eight notes   a - part.
2. Tune   your   4th   fin - ger   with   your   o - pen   G.

Play   them   each   day,   it's   a   great   way   to   start.
Play   it   and   make those   Gs   match per - fect - ly.

The sharps at the start of the music are called **key signatures**.

26

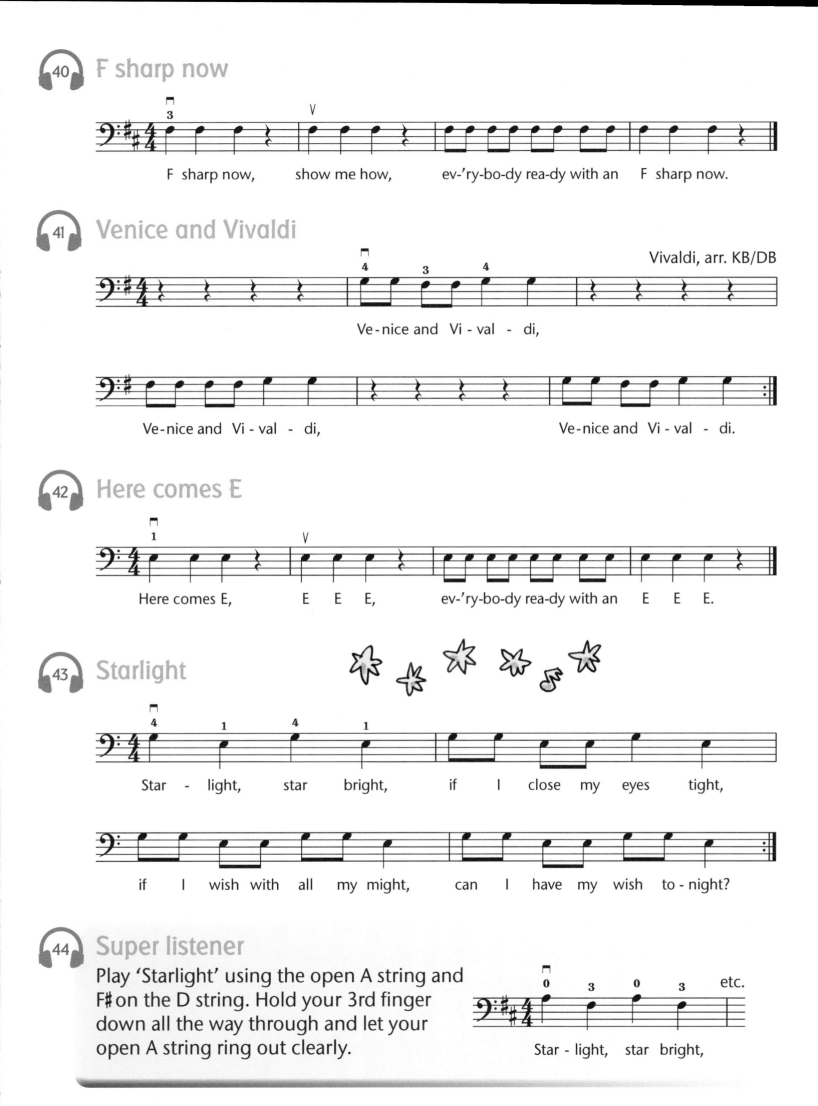

40 F sharp now

F sharp now, show me how, ev-'ry-bo-dy rea-dy with an F sharp now.

41 Venice and Vivaldi

Vivaldi, arr. KB/DB

Ve - nice and Vi - val - di,

Ve - nice and Vi - val - di, Ve - nice and Vi - val - di.

42 Here comes E

Here comes E, E E E, ev-'ry-bo-dy rea-dy with an E E E.

43 Starlight

Star - light, star bright, if I close my eyes tight,

if I wish with all my might, can I have my wish to - night?

44 Super listener

Play 'Starlight' using the open A string and F♯ on the D string. Hold your 3rd finger down all the way through and let your open A string ring out clearly.

etc.

Star - light, star bright,

D-string activity page

Writing time

Draw these D-string notes on the stave below:

Bar 1: ♩ x 4 on open D

Bar 2: ♩ x 2 on E

Bar 3: ♩ ❩ ♩ ❩ on F♯

Bar 4: ♩ on G and a two-beat rest

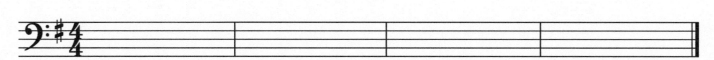

Now draw a down-bow sign above the first note and play the tune through.

Roller coaster quiz

Play 'Roller coaster' on page 24 and then do the quiz below.

Speed - ing   rol - ler   coast - er,   spin - ning   me   a - round.   I'm

feel - ing   ve - ry   diz - zy   so   far   from   the ground.

- Some notes are missing in the tune. Fill them in where you see the * sign.

- Draw a circle around the time signature.

- Fill in the missing number: 4/4 means _____ ♩ beats in a bar.

- A ♩ rest is missing in bar 4. Draw it in correctly.

- Draw a circle around some ♫ Es.

- How many F♯s can you count in the first line? _____

28

D-string tunes

Fit as a fiddle

Play the rhythm variations in verses 2 and 3 and end each verse with the chorus.

Verse 1

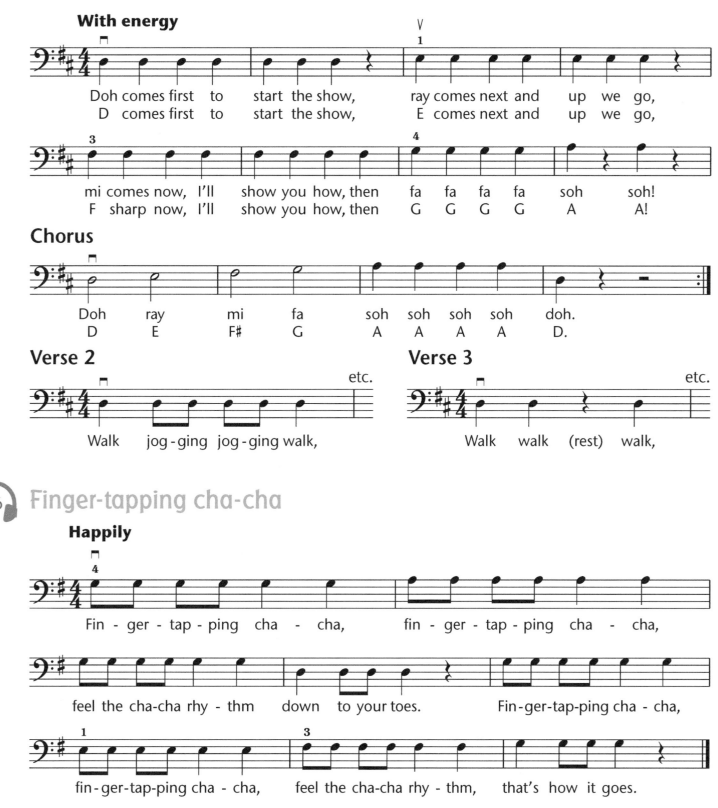

Finger-tapping cha-cha

Chant this as you tap your left-hand 4th finger on the string:

Tap your finger, wiggle your thumb. Tap your finger, wiggle your thumb. Tap your finger, wiggle your thumb. Let's get ready, now here it comes. (*repeat the piece*)

Lost shoe blues

Play with a swing

G I'm blue, lost my shoe, don't know where I put it, got the

lost shoe blues. I'll miss the bus, what a fuss!

late for school and teach-er's mad, I feel so sad. I'll have to hop,

trem.

and not stop, don't know where I put it, got the lost shoe blues.

The next piece is in $\frac{2}{4}$.
What do you think that means?

Missed it!

On the move

Run-ning to the rail-way sta-tion, hope the train will be on time. I've

checked the time and des-tin-a-tion, it's on plat-form nine. Oh!

Train went past, it left with-out me, sped right down that rail-way line. I'm

stand-ing here at plat-form one, not plat-form num-ber nine!

At the end of the piece, slide your left hand up and down the fingerboard like a fast train.

A-string notes

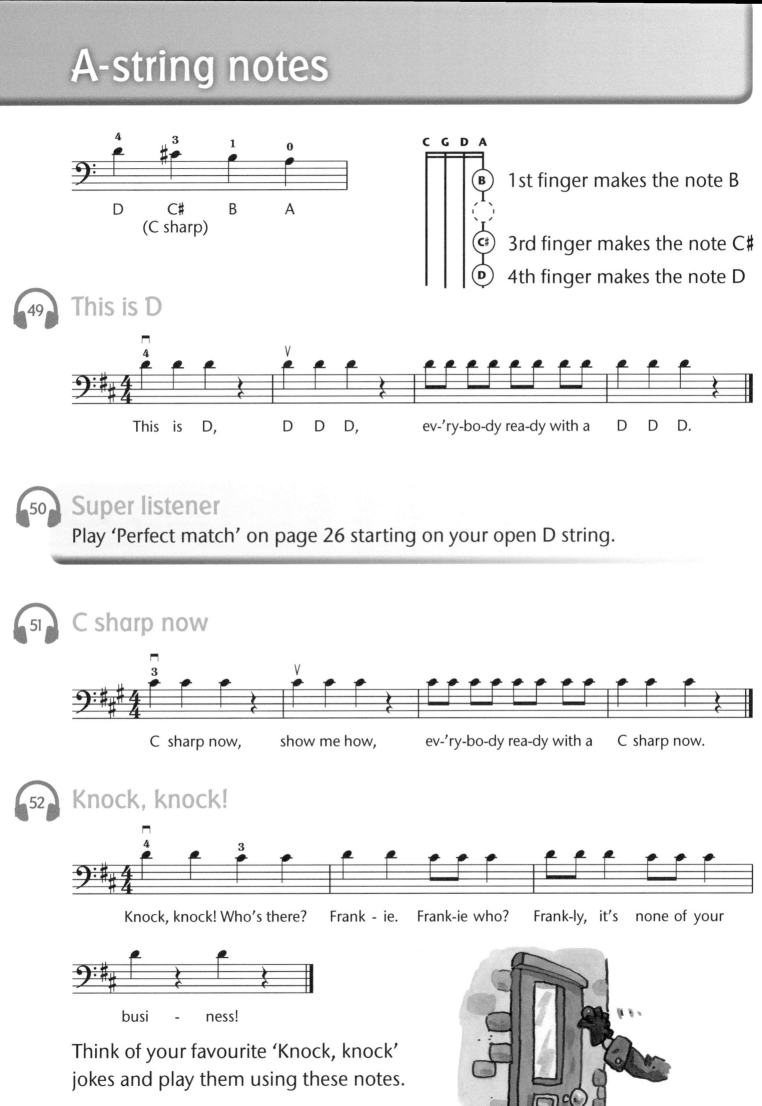

D C# B A
(C sharp)

C G D A

B 1st finger makes the note B

C# 3rd finger makes the note C#

D 4th finger makes the note D

49 This is D

This   is   D,   D   D   D,   ev-'ry-bo-dy rea-dy with a   D   D   D.

50 Super listener

Play 'Perfect match' on page 26 starting on your open D string.

51 C sharp now

C sharp now,   show me how,   ev-'ry-bo-dy rea-dy with a   C sharp now.

52 Knock, knock!

Knock, knock! Who's there?   Frank - ie.   Frank-ie who?   Frank-ly, it's   none of your

busi - ness!

Think of your favourite 'Knock, knock'
jokes and play them using these notes.

31

53 **Here comes B**

Here comes B, B B B, ev-'ry-bo-dy rea-dy with a B B B.

Have you got a good left-hand position? Keep checking!

54 **Off to school**

On the go

Friends and I, we walk to school, we walk walk walk walk,

that's our rule. Walk walk walk walk walk walk walk.

Then when it's time to go home from school, we're jog-ging jog-ging jog-ging jog-ging,

Slower l.h. pizz.

that's our rule! Jog-ging jog-ging jog-ging jog-ging. Phew let's stop!

* Tap your 4th finger on the A string.

55 **Wake up!**

Insistent

Wake up in the morn - in', got - ta stop your snor - in',

wake up in the morn - in', wake up! Here's your fi - nal warn - in',

got - ta stop your yawn - in', here's your fi - nal warn - in', get up!

32

Writing time

Draw the A-string notes on the stave below. Each note will be a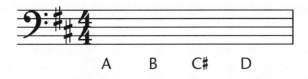

A   B   C#   D

Be an A-string composer

Use the rhythm shown to write your own tune using the A-string notes. Choose one note per bar.

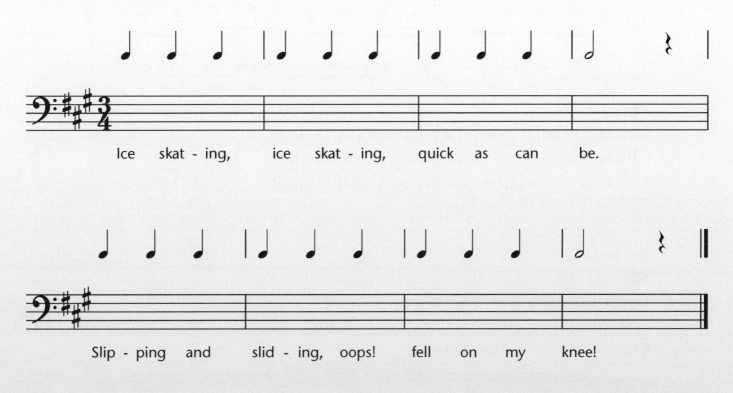

Ice   skat - ing,   ice   skat - ing,   quick   as   can   be.

Slip - ping   and   slid - ing, oops!   fell   on   my   knee!

Now draw a down-bow sign above the first note and play your tune through.

33

A-string tunes

56 Get aboard

Try some swinging rhythms in verses 2 and 3. Listen to track 56 to hear how it goes and get the swing of it!

Verse 1

Get a-board the rhy-thm train, we're head-ing out of town, yeah.

Get a-board the rhy-thm train for we're Chi-ca-go bound.

Verse 2

Chickety-can, it goes speeding along, it goes
Chickety-can, it goes speeding along, it goes
Chickety-can, it goes speeding along, it goes
Chickety-can all day long!

Verse 3

Speeding here and speeding there, it
Speeds right down the railway track, it's
Speeding here and speeding there, don't
Know when we'll be back!

57 Clear blue sky

Gently

x3

1. Come and fly, way up high, we will see clear blue sky.
2. Like a bird fly-ing round, soar-ing far from the ground.
3. Fly-ing high on the wing, see them swoop, hear them sing.

34

Harmonic-ky things

Octave harmonics: to find this special sound, touch the string very lightly about halfway along with your 3rd finger. This is the harmonic sign: ○

Harmonic-ky thing

Emma's lullaby

Can you find the octave harmonic on the C string?

Clear blue sky

Play this harmonic part while your friend or teacher plays the tune on the opposite page, then swap over. Use audio track 57.

Scale builder

Scale-y dragon

Choose an idea from the scale-y dragon and play a scale of D major in that way. Make up some more ideas of your own.

Scale of D major

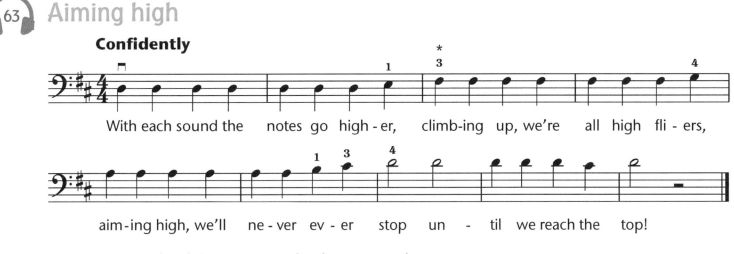

Play a different rhythm for each note of the scale.

Play 4/4 rhythms with track 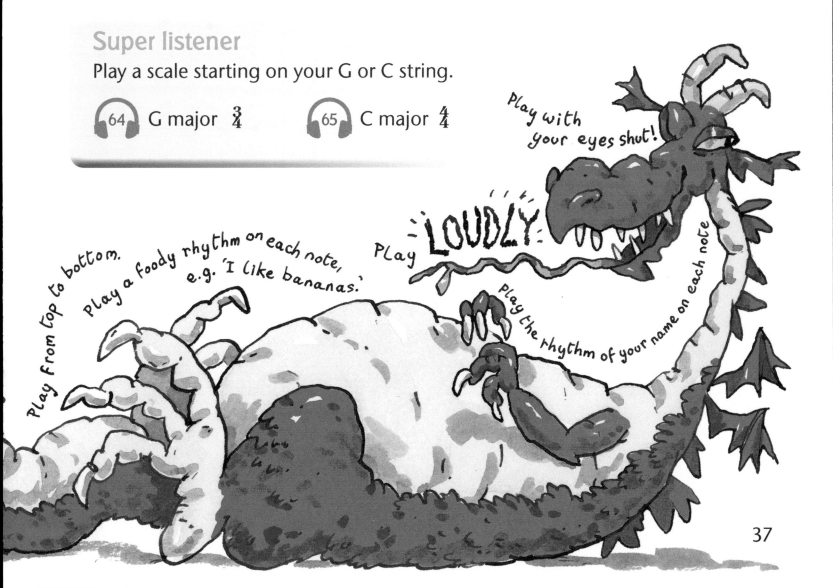61. Play 3/4 rhythms with track 62.

63 Aiming high

Confidently

With each sound the notes go high - er, climb-ing up, we're all high fli - ers,

aim-ing high, we'll ne - ver ev - er stop un - til we reach the top!

Play 'Aiming high' as a round. The second part enters at *.

Super listener

Play a scale starting on your G or C string.

64 G major 3/4   65 C major 4/4

Play with your eyes shut!

Play from top to bottom.

Play a foody rhythm on each note, e.g. 'I like bananas.'

Play LOUDLY.

Play the rhythm of your name on each note

37

Show tunes

Soualle

Like a lullaby

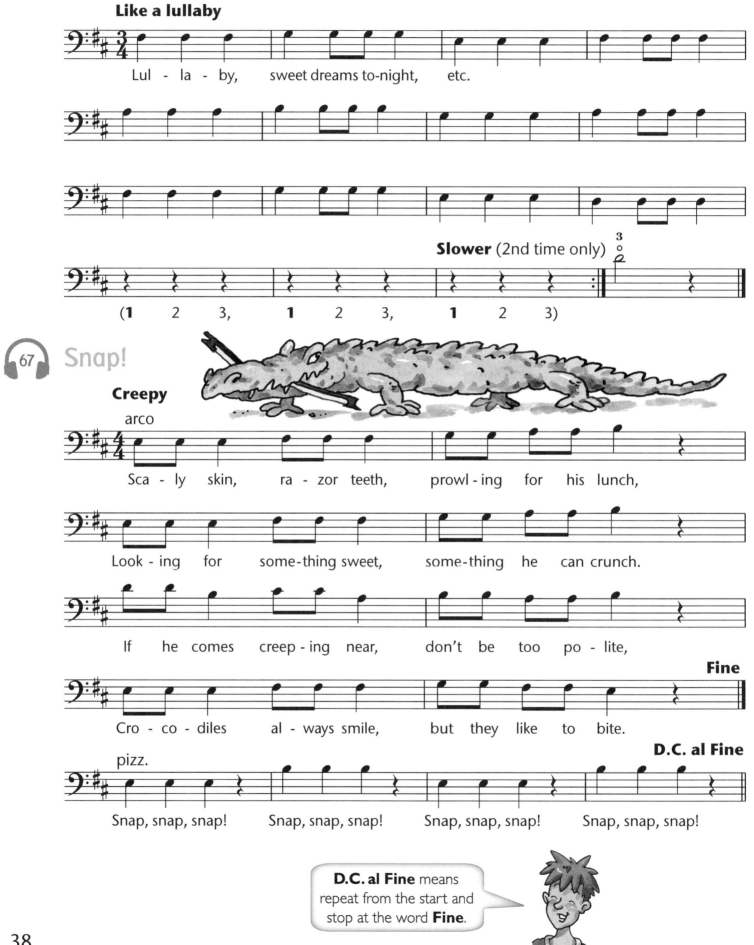

Lul - la - by, sweet dreams to-night, etc.

Slower (2nd time only)

(**1** 2 3, **1** 2 3, **1** 2 3)

67 Snap!

Creepy

arco

Sca - ly skin, ra - zor teeth, prowl - ing for his lunch,

Look - ing for some-thing sweet, some-thing he can crunch.

If he comes creep - ing near, don't be too po - lite,

Fine

Cro - co - diles al - ways smile, but they like to bite.

pizz.

D.C. al Fine

Snap, snap, snap! Snap, snap, snap! Snap, snap, snap! Snap, snap, snap!

D.C. al Fine means repeat from the start and stop at the word **Fine**.

38

More Mini Mozart

Gracefully

Mo - zart wrote mu - sic he played on the pia - no, he

wrote lots of tunes and he played all day long.

Try these rhythm variations:

Walk jog-ging walk, walk jog-ging walk, etc.

Walk jog-ging jog-ging, walk jog-ging jog-ging, etc.

Hide and seek

On the move

Run - ning round the play - ground, look - ing for my friends, I

just can't find them here, it's hide and seek a-gain, I think that I spy some-one

hid-ing o - ver there, but oops there goes the bell, it's just not fair!

Happily

Sum-mer's here, the sun is shin-ing bright - ly, time to have a ho - li -

- day. Blue skies, blue sea, sand be-tween my toes, and

ice-cream on the beach to - day! Sum - mer's here, the

sun is shin-ing bright - ly, I just love the ho - li - days, yes I do!